# EXPLORING COUNTRIES

# Taiwan

by Lisa Owings

BLASTOFF!
READERS
5

BELLWETHER MEDIA • MINNEAPOLIS, MN

Note to Librarians, Teachers, and Parents:

**Blastoff! Readers** are carefully developed by literacy experts and combine standards-based content with developmentally appropriate text.

**Level 1** provides the most support through repetition of high-frequency words, light text, predictable sentence patterns, and strong visual support.

**Level 2** offers early readers a bit more challenge through varied simple sentences, increased text load, and less repetition of high-frequency words.

**Level 3** advances early-fluent readers toward fluency through increased text and concept load, less reliance on visuals, longer sentences, and more literary language.

**Level 4** builds reading stamina by providing more text per page, increased use of punctuation, greater variation in sentence patterns, and increasingly challenging vocabulary.

**Level 5** encourages children to move from "learning to read" to "reading to learn" by providing even more text, varied writing styles, and less familiar topics.

Whichever book is right for your reader, Blastoff! Readers are the perfect books to build confidence and encourage a love of reading that will last a lifetime!

This edition first published in 2014 by Bellwether Media, Inc.

No part of this publication may be reproduced in whole or in part without written permission of the publisher. For information regarding permission, write to Bellwether Media, Inc., Attention: Permissions Department, 5357 Penn Avenue South, Minneapolis, MN 55419.

Library of Congress Cataloging-in-Publication Data

Owings, Lisa.
  Taiwan / by Lisa Owings.
     pages cm. – (Blastoff! Readers: Exploring Countries)
  Includes bibliographical references and index.
  Summary: "Developed by literacy experts for students in grades three through seven, this book introduces young readers to the geography and culture of Taiwan"– Provided by publisher.
  ISBN 978-1-62617-070-4 (hardcover : alk. paper)
  1. Taiwan–Juvenile literature.  I. Title.
  DS799.O94 2014
  951.249–dc23
                                              2013035878

Printed in the United States of America, North Mankato, MN.

# Contents

The island of Taiwan sits about 100 miles (160 kilometers) off China's southeastern coast. Pacific Ocean waves crash against the eastern mountains. The Luzon **Strait** separates Taiwan from the Philippines in the south. Along the island's western coast, the Taiwan Strait stretches between the East and South China Seas. A few islands in surrounding waters also belong to Taiwan.

The capital city of Taipei is in northern Taiwan. Taipei is home to the **Republic** of China (ROC). This government once ruled all of China. In 1949, a different government called the People's Republic of China (PRC) forced it out and took over China. The ROC fled to Taiwan. Today, Taiwan governs itself under the ROC. However, many countries recognize the island as a part of the PRC.

**China**

**Did you know?**
Taiwan was once known as
*Ilha Formosa,* or "beautiful
island." Portuguese sailors
gave it that name after
visiting in 1590.

**East
China Sea**

**Taiwan
Strait**

★
**Taipei**

**Pacific
Ocean**

**Taiwan**

**South
China Sea**

**Luzon Strait**

**Philippine
Sea**

**Plains** and gentle hills cover western Taiwan. The land is a patchwork of cities and farms. Wind and waves shape the **dunes** and beaches along the Taiwan Strait. Eastern Taiwan is rugged and mountainous. The forested peaks of the Chung-yang Range run the length of the island from north to south. They include Taiwan's highest point, Yü Shan. The mountains extend to the east coast, where they rise steeply above the Pacific Ocean.

Dozens of rivers flow from the mountains to the sea. During the warm summer months, **typhoons** sometimes cause them to overflow their banks. Winters are brief but cool, with snow falling in the mountains.

**Did you know?**
Earthquakes occur often in Taiwan. One of the deadliest shook central Taiwan in 1999. Around 2,400 people were killed.

People travel from all over the world to visit Taroko National Park in northeastern Taiwan. Its most stunning feature is the Taroko **Gorge**. The Liwu River rushes through the bottom of the gorge. Steep cliffs of pale marble rise on either side. The river carves the stone into a hauntingly beautiful landscape.

High above the river, the mountains are crowned with lush forests and waterfalls. **Tourists** admire the view from bridges and trails cut into the cliffs. Lucky visitors might spot a few colorful birds or pink-faced monkeys as they hike. Many stop for a dip in the river.

Liwu River

# Did you know?

The Eternal Spring Shrine sits above one of Taroko's waterfalls. Perched on a cliff, this building honors those who died while constructing a major highway nearby.

Formosan rock macaque

Much of Taiwan's wildlife is unique to the island. The **Formosan** black bear **forages** for food in mountain forests. Grassy hillsides attract deer such as Formosan sambars. The goat-like Formosan serow can be seen leaping over mountain slopes. Forest **canopies** shelter Formosan rock macaques and flying squirrels.

hawksbill sea turtle

blue magpie

Formosan sambar

## fun fact

Every spring and fall, thousands of purple crow butterflies can be seen flying over Taiwan. They spend winters in southern Taiwan and summers in northern Taiwan.

Taiwan's skies are filled with birds and butterflies. The blue magpie spreads its long feathers as it flies. Mikado and Swinhoe's pheasants strut across the ground. Birdwing butterflies show off their colors as they flit between flowers. Off the coast, humpback whales, bottlenose dolphins, and hawksbill sea turtles surface to breathe.

**Did you know?**
Mandarin Chinese is a tonal language. The meaning of a word can change depending on if the sound of your voice is high, low, rising, or falling.

Taiwan is home to more than 23 million people. Most of them have Chinese **ancestors**. In the 1600s, Chinese began to move to Taiwan. More than eight out of every ten Taiwanese **descend** from these settlers. A smaller group of Chinese came to the island in the late 1940s. The tiny number of **native** Taiwanese live mainly in the eastern mountains.

Mandarin Chinese is Taiwan's official language. A variety of other Chinese **dialects** and native languages are also spoken. Many Taiwanese value Buddhist, Taoist, and **traditional** religions equally. Islanders are known for being polite and friendly. They go out of their way to help visitors feel at home.

# Speak Mandarin!

Mandarin is written in characters. However, Mandarin words can be written in English to help you read them out loud.

| English | Mandarin | How to say it |
| --- | --- | --- |
| hello | ni hao | NEE how |
| good-bye | zai jian | ZA-ee JEN |
| yes | shi | shr |
| no | bu shi | BOO shr |
| please | qing | ching |
| thank you | xie-xie | SHEH sheh |
| friend | peng-you | peng-YO |

**Did you know?**
In the evenings, many Taiwanese in cities gather at open-air markets. These night markets feature bright lights and stall after stall of delicious foods and other goods.

Taiwan is a crowded island. Most Taiwanese make their homes in the cities of western Taiwan. Families generally live in small apartments. In large cities such as Taipei, bright signs advertise rows of shops and restaurants. The streets are packed with cars, taxis, and motorcycles.

In the countryside, many families live in small houses made of brick. Extended families often live together in the same home. People ride bicycles or scooters into the nearest town to go shopping. They can also stop by a local shop or market. More and more Taiwanese are leaving the countryside to live in the city.

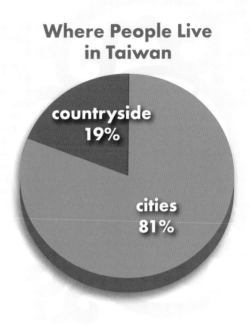

**Where People Live in Taiwan**

countryside 19%

cities 81%

## Did you know?

After the regular school day, many Taiwanese teens attend cram schools until late in the evening. The extra studying is thought to help them improve their test scores.

School is the main focus of Taiwanese children's lives. They attend school for at least nine years, starting at age 6. The first six years are spent in primary school. Students learn Mandarin, science, and math. At home, parents help their children with schoolwork. Children study harder during the three years of middle school. At the end, all students take an exam. They must do well to move on to high school.

High school is also stressful. Students face a lot of pressure to get into a good college. Taiwanese teens spend most of their free time studying for college entrance exams. Most attend one of the more than 100 colleges and universities in Taiwan.

## Where People Work in Taiwan

manufacturing 36.2%

services 58.8%

farming 5%

Much of Taiwan's income is from selling goods made on the island to countries around the world. In cities, skilled factory workers produce high-tech electronics and machinery. They also make clothing, metals, and chemicals. Taiwanese with **service jobs** often work in small, family-owned shops and restaurants. Others work in schools, banks, and hotels.

In Taiwan's countryside, farmers tend crops of rice and tea. Many also grow fruits and vegetables such as bananas, pineapples, and asparagus. Some workers bring up oil, natural gas, and marble from the earth. Others chop down trees for wood. In coastal waters, fishers catch tuna, eels, and sea snails.

Taiwanese are crazy about baseball. Children join Little Leagues and adults root for the Chinese Taipei national baseball team. Families enjoy attending games or watching them on television. Many Taiwanese also play basketball or practice the **martial art** of *tai chi*. In native villages, singing and dancing help keep traditions alive.

Young Taiwanese love to visit with friends. They head to the movies, go shopping, or gather at bubble tea stands to chat. They also keep in touch over the Internet. Families enjoy **scenic** hikes through national parks. Beaches and **hot springs** are favorite places to relax. Many Taiwanese vacation in China, Japan, or other nearby countries.

## Did you know?

Sweet potatoes are especially loved in Taiwan because they have the same shape as the island.

Taiwanese love food so much that they greet each other with, "Have you eaten?" Rice, seafood, and vegetables are featured in many dishes. *Lu rou fan*, or rice with braised pork, is a national favorite. Beef noodle soup is another classic. Oysters are added to omelets or eaten in oyster vermicelli, a soupy noodle dish.

Snacking is a passion in Taiwan. *Siao chih*, or "small eats," are found at night markets. Taiwanese feast on steamed buns filled with pork and gravy-smothered dumplings called *bawan*. Chewy eggs cooked in soy sauce and stinky tofu are other favorite treats. Beloved sweets include pineapple cakes and mounds of shaved ice.

## fun fact

A meaty dish called Buddha Jumps Over the Wall is said to be so good that even the most rigid vegetarian would sneak a bite. It has more than 30 ingredients, including shark fin!

steamed buns

Buddha Jumps Over the Wall

Ghost Festival

The Taiwanese begin each year of celebrations with Chinese New Year in January or February. People get together with family and chat over the sounds of firecrackers. Lion and dragon dancers parade through the streets in showy costumes. Late summer brings the month-long Ghost Festival, when the dead are said to wander the island. People prepare food and offerings for the ghosts of their ancestors.

The Moon Festival comes in mid-autumn. Families and friends gather for barbecues under the full moon. Everyone feasts on pomelo fruits and moon cakes. October 10 is Republic Day in Taiwan. It celebrates the day when China became a republic. Festivities include a large parade and fireworks.

Did you know?
The Dragon Boat Festival is held in Taiwan each summer. People watch dragon boat races and drop rice dumplings into the water.

## Did you know?

Taiwanese serve some types of tea in tall cups called aroma cups. Guests transfer the tea into a smaller cup, and then enjoy the scent captured in the aroma cup.

**aroma cup**

Tea is a way of life in Taiwan. The island is famous for growing high-quality *oolong* teas. Rows of tea bushes curve over the mountain slopes. Taiwanese drink tea constantly. They offer it to guests and serve it during weddings. Friends meet at teahouses, sipping while they talk or play games. Tea stands sell cold, sweet bubble tea. The "bubbles" are balls of chewy tapioca.

The beauty of Taiwanese tea is best appreciated through *gongfu cha*, the Chinese tea ceremony. Tea is carefully prepared and served to guests in small cups. The guests admire the color and scent of the tea before drinking it. Tea helps Taiwanese remember their history, strengthen friendships, and find peace.

**fun fact**
Every kind of tea is made from the same plant, *camellia sinensis*.

# Fast Facts About Taiwan

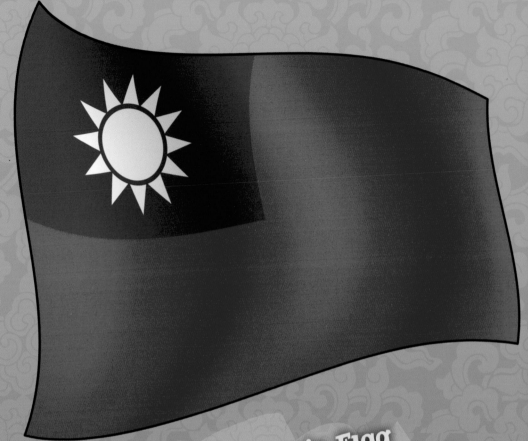

## Taiwan's Flag

The red flag of Taiwan has a blue rectangle in the upper left corner. Inside the rectangle is a white sun. The red stands for national pride and sacrifice. The blue represents freedom and democracy. The white sun symbolizes equality and progress. Taiwan's flag was adopted in 1928.

**Official Name:** Republic of China

**Area:** 13,892 square miles (35,980 square kilometers); Taiwan is the 139th largest country in the world.

| | |
|---|---|
| **Capital City:** | Taipei |
| **Important Cities:** | Kaohsiung, Taichung, Tainan |
| **Population:** | 23,299,716 (July 2013) |
| **Official Language:** | Mandarin Chinese |
| **National Holiday:** | Republic Day (October 10) |
| **Religions:** | Mixture of Buddhist and Taoist (93%), Christian (4.5%), other (2.5%) |
| **Major Industries:** | manufacturing, farming, fishing, services |
| **Natural Resources:** | oil, natural gas, coal, marble, limestone |
| **Manufactured Products:** | electronics, machinery, metals, chemicals, textiles, food products |
| **Farm Products:** | rice, tropical fruits, sugarcane, tea, flowers, fish, chicken, pork |
| **Unit of Money:** | New Taiwan dollar; the New Taiwan dollar is divided into 100 cents. |

# Glossary

**ancestors**—relatives who lived long ago

**canopies**—thick coverings of leafy branches formed by the tops of trees

**descend**—to be related to a group of ancestors

**dialects**—unique ways of speaking a language; dialects are often specific to certain regions of a country.

**dunes**—hills of sand

**forages**—searches for food

**Formosan**—relating to Taiwan's land, people, or language

**gorge**—a deep, narrow valley with steep, rocky sides

**hot springs**—areas of hot water that flows up through cracks in the earth

**martial art**—a style or technique of fighting and self-defense

**native**—originally from a specific place

**plains**—large areas of flat land

**republic**—a nation ruled by elected leaders instead of a king or queen

**scenic**—providing beautiful views of the natural surroundings

**service jobs**—jobs that perform tasks for people or businesses

**strait**—a narrow stretch of water that connects two larger bodies of water

**tourists**—people who travel to visit another place

**traditional**—relating to a custom, idea, or belief handed down from one generation to the next

**typhoons**—severe rotating storms that form over warm seas in the northwestern Pacific Ocean

# To Learn More

**AT THE LIBRARY**

Behnke, Alison. *Taiwan in Pictures*. Minneapolis, Minn.: Twenty-First Century Books, 2008.

Nardo, Don. *Buddhism*. Minneapolis, Minn.: Compass Point Books, 2009.

Simonds, Nina. *Moonbeams, Dumplings, and Dragon Boats: A Treasury of Chinese Holiday Tales, Activities, and Recipes*. San Diego, Calif.: Harcourt, Inc., 2002.

**ON THE WEB**

Learning more about Taiwan is as easy as 1, 2, 3.

1. Go to www.factsurfer.com.

2. Enter "Taiwan" into the search box.

3. Click the "Surf" button and you will see a list of related Web sites.

With factsurfer.com, finding more information is just a click away.

# Index